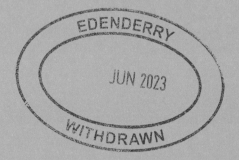
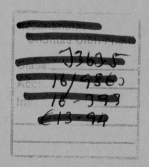

Wants versus Needs

A Place to Live

Linda Staniford

raintree

a Capstone company — publishers for children

Raintree is an imprint of Capstone Global Library Limited, a company incorporated in England and Wales having its registered office at 7 Pilgrim Street, London, EC4V 6LB – Registered company number: 6695582

www.raintreepublishers.co.uk
myorders@raintreepublishers.co.uk

Edited by Linda Staniford and Shelly Lyons
Designed by Philippa Jenkins
Original illustrations © Capstone Global Library Ltd 2015
Picture research by Tracy Cummins
Production by Helen McCreath
Originated by Capstone Global Library Ltd
Printed and bound in China

ISBN 978 1 406 29058 5
18 17 16 15 14
10 9 8 7 6 5 4 3 2 1

British Library Cataloguing in Publication Data
A full catalogue record for this book is available from the British Library.

Acknowledgements
We would like to thank the following for permission to reproduce photographs: Capstone Press: Philippa Jenkins, Cover Left, Design Elements; Getty Images: BLOOM image, 15, Britain On View, 16, Pauline St.Denis, 17, Vesnaandjic, 7, 23; Shutterstock: Kotomiti Okuma, 12, 22 BL, alexmisu, 4, Andrejs Zavadskis, 5, Andresr, 21, Chinaview, 10, Golden Pixels LLC, 9, Monkey Business Images, 14, 18, 20, 23, Radek Sturgolewski, Back Cover, Renata Osinska, 8, 22 TL, 23, Sergey Nivens, 1, Cover Right, Tatyana Vyc, 11, 22 TR, 23, WDG Photo, 6; Thinkstock: Jupiterimages, 13, 19, 22 BR, 23.

Every effort has been made to contact copyright holders of material reproduced in this book. Any omissions will be rectified in subsequent printings if notice is given to the publisher.

Contents

Some words are shown in bold, **like this**. You can find them in the glossary on page 23.

What are needs and wants?

Needs are things we must have to survive. Everyone needs a place to live. If you have a big family, you may need to live in a big house.

Wants are things we would like to have.
You might want to live in a palace, but
you do not need to!

Why do we need shelter?

Our homes keep us safe. We need to keep warm and dry. Our homes keep out the wind and rain. They protect us from bad weather.

Our home gives us **shelter**. Shelter is a place where you feel safe. It is important to feel safe in your home.

How do our homes make us feel comfortable?

We need to feel **comfortable** in our home. We need a bed to sleep in. We also need chairs to sit in while reading or for our friends to sit in when they visit.

If your friend has a big comfy sofa, you might want a big sofa too. But you do not need to have exactly the same things as they do.

9

What do we need for cooking food?

In our home, we need a kitchen with a cooker. We need pots and pans to cook food in. What else do you think you need in a kitchen?

It is fun to have lots of whizzy kitchen **gadgets**, such as a juice maker. But you do not need them.

What do we need to keep clean?

We need to keep clean. We need a bathroom with a sink and a bath or shower to wash in. What else do you think we need in the bathroom?

You might want bubble bath and rubber ducks in your bathroom. But you do not need these things.

How do we keep warm or cool in our homes?

We need to keep warm in winter. Different homes have different kinds of **heating**. Some homes have radiators. Some homes have fires.

In summer we need to keep cool
in our home. We can use fans or
air conditioning.

Where do we need to live?

Some families live in towns or cities. They need to live near their work. They like to live where there are lots of people.

Some families live in the country. They need to be near their work. They like to be outdoors. All families need to live where they feel **comfortable**.

What do we need outside our homes?

We need somewhere to play outside and get fresh air and **exercise**. You could go to a park. You can play in the playground with your friends.

You might be lucky and have a garden where you live. It can be fun to play games on the grass or sit and chat with friends.

Who else lives in our homes?

We cannot live on our own until we are grown-ups. We need to be with adults who will look after us and care for us.

We might also want to have pets to look after and to play with. Our pets need us to care for them!

Quiz

Which of these things are wants and which are needs?

Picture glossary

comfortable feeling at ease

exercise activity to keep your body strong

gadget tool with a clever or unusual use

heating way of keeping warm

shelter place where we feel safe

Index

Note to parents and teachers

Reading non-fiction texts for information is an important part of a child's literary development. Readers can be encouraged to ask simple questions and then use the text to find the answers. Each chapter in this book begins with a question. Read the questions together. Look at the pictures. Talk about what the answer might be. Then read the text to find out if your predictions were correct. To develop readers' enquiry skills, encourage them to think of other questions they might ask about the topic. Discuss where you could find the answers. Assist children in using the contents page, picture glossary and index to practise research skills and new vocabulary.